FROM THE **MUSIC POWER** SERIES

DANCE HITS THROUGH THE DECADES

Introduction by John Jacobson • Lesson Plans by Tom Anderson

Table of Contents

HAL•LEONARD® CORPORATION
7777 W. BLUEMOUND RD. P.O. BOX 13819 MILWAUKEE, WI 53213

Visit Hal Leonard Online at
www.halleonard.com

Introduction & Staging Suggestions

By John Jacobson

Artists know that history is best reflected in the artistic endeavors of its time. The music and poetry, the paintings and sculptures, the literature and theatrical works and more remind us of who we were as a human race and a society. Not only do they give us clues as to who we were, but often great works of art can even foretell a sense of where we all might be going in the future. Believe it or not, nowhere is this more true than in the popular dances of most all periods of our history. Want to learn about Italian Renaissance in the 15th and 16th Century? Watch an historical dance company perform a Pavane, a Salterello or a Galliard. Interested in how people acted in the Baroque French courts of 17th and 18th Century? Learn to do a Minuet, an Allemande or a Gigue. When you do a Waltz, a Polka or a Quadrille, you are dancing like the members of 19th Century English and American high society. When you execute the Fox Trot, the Tango, the Charleston, Swing Dance or even the Twist, you have finally made it to the Twentieth Century of American Dance reflecting the ups and downs, dips and unexpected curves of life right here in America. That's where this celebration **Dance Hits Through The Decades** really begins!

In this collection of hits, we have included choral arrangements of popular songs that were written and recorded to be danced to. In addition, there are Fun Facts and additional trivia from the '50s through the '80s, along with helpful Lesson Plans and activities for each decade song. Let me take you through each of these selections and remind you of a few of the accompanying dances that you might incorporate into the performance of these tunes, keeping in mind that most of these songs were written for an ensemble to sing and party-goers to dance. Each of the dances we mention here will work well even when the singers and the dancers are one and the same. After all, nothing is more uniquely American than the great combination that is song and dance.

50s Rock Around The Clock

World War II is finally behind us. Rock and Roll is born and thriving. Fast cars, slicked-back hair, poodle skirts and saddle shoes ... its time to *Rock Around the Clock* tonight!

Here are four dances from the 1950s that work swell in the performance of "Rock Around the Clock."

1. The Twist

Chubby Checker did our waistlines a big favor when he introduced us to the Twist in the 1950s.

Basic Twist: Stand on the balls of your feet and twist your heels from side to side so that you twist at the waist. Use your arms to move in opposition.

Variations of the Basic Twist:

- Try leaning to the left for eight counts, then to the right for eight counts as you twist.
- Twist while bending your knees so you squat to the floor in eight counts then twist back to standing up straight.

• 8-Count Twist: Facing the audience the entire time with shoulders square to them,

(1) Twist at the waist and bring right knee across the front and to the left as the upper body (especially arms) twists to the right.
(2-3) Lower that right knee and twist both knees right/left.
(4) raise left knee across the front to the right as upper body twists left.
(5-6) Twist lower body left/right.
(7) Repeat the right knee across front as in beat 1.
(8) Lower right leg.

Repeat the entire eight counts again starting once more with the right leg across.

Since a picture or video is worth a thousand words, and perhaps a million when it comes to dance, check out Definition #99 in John Jacobson's DICTIONARY OF DANCE for a live demonstration of the 8-Count Twist.

This pattern would work great at the first verse of the song where you begin singing *"Put your bright lights on ..."*

2. **Six-Count Jitterbug** (definition #203 in DICTIONARY OF DANCE)

Although we usually think of a Jitterbug as a partnered dance, this particular pattern can be performed with or without a dance partner for effective song and dance.

With knees turned out:

(1-2) Step L followed by a ball change (RL).
(3-4) Step R followed by a ball change (LR).
(5-6) Back step (LR).

If you started the dance on beat one of a four-beat measure, the accented L foot will be on a different beat of each ensuing measure until you have made an entire round of 24 counts. If this is performed with a partner in a traditional ballroom dance position, the female dancer would begin the combination stepping onto the R foot.

3. **The Lindy** (Definition #226 in DICTIONARY OF DANCE)

This is a five-step move that takes four counts to complete. A basic Lindy step consists of a Chassé (slide to one side) followed by a backstep. For instance, slide to the L in a dotted eighth-sixteenth-quarter pattern (LRL) and then a two quarter note back step (RL), keeping your shoulders square to the audience the entire time. Like the six-count Jitterbug, The Lindy can be performed with a partner in a traditional Ballroom Dance Position (Definition #24).

4. **The Hand Jive** (Definition #155 in DICTIONARY OF DANCE)

This involces a 16-count clapping pattern that is fun, easy, and perfectly reflective of the upbeat dances of the 1950s.

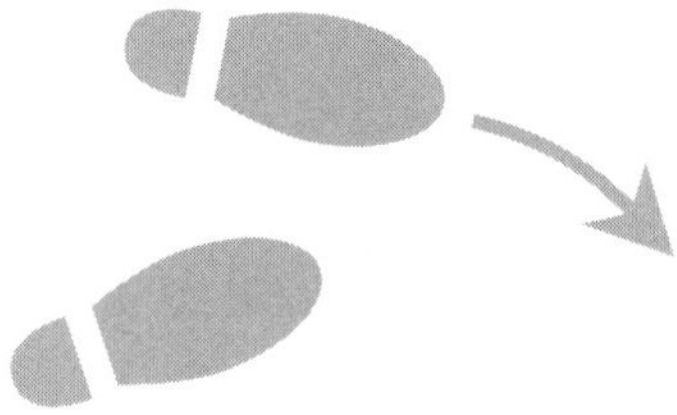

(1-2) Slap your thighs two times.

(3-4) Clap twice.

(5-6) Slice your R hand two times over your L in a scissoring move.

(7-8) Slice your L hand two times over your R in a scissoring move.

(9-10) Pound your R fist on top of your L fist two times.

(11-12) Pound your L fist over your R fist two times.

(13-14) Accent your R thumb over your R shoulder like a hitchhike, two times.

(15-16) Accent your L thumb over your L shoulder like a hitchhike, two times.

Spice the Hand Jive up a bit by step touching in time with the music as you do it.

60s The Loco-motion

"The Loco-motion" was a song and a specific dance, much like Chubby Checker's The Twist from the 1950s.

The Loco-motion dance is made up of two basic parts.

1. **Train Arms:** (Definition #425) With 90-degree bent elbows, churn them at your sides like the wheels of an old-fashioned railroad train.

2. **Heel Drags:** A bit of a misnomer in that the 'heel' is not being dragged so much as the whole of the opposite foot. It is a move that begins by stepping onto the heel of one foot with the toes in the air (for example, out to the L), then pulling the opposite foot (R) along so that the feet come together. In other words, the pattern of this walking pattern is step (heel), 'drag' in the opposite foot.

Now combine the Train Arms and the Heel Drags. Try it four times moving in one direction when you sing the words *"Come on baby do the Locomotion"*. Then four in the other direction when you sing that again.

70s Y.M.C.A.

Trying to explain "Y.M.C.A." is like trying to tell young people that you question their taste in clothes and then they show you a picture of yourself in wide bell bottoms, hip huggers and love beads! Best to just let it go and have a lot of fun. The '70s did give us Disco which is rearing its head again in this new century, so it must be here to stay.

My favorite way to stage "Y.M.C.A." is to incorporate some of your favorite gym calisthenics.

Stylized Alternating Toe Touchers: (Definition #9) Stand with your feet apart and with arms outstretched at shoulder level. Bend at your waist so that your right hand reaches to touch your left foot. Then stand upright. Now bend at the waist so that your left hand touches your right foot. Now modify it in ways that allow you do simulate it but still sing.

Deep Knee Bends, Chain Breakers, even Jumping Jacks and Push Ups can be used to set up the scenario of the "Y.M.C.A."

Partner Disco: The easiest Disco step is to stand with a partner in ballroom dance position and simply walk smoothly in a circle around each other. The female dancer will be walking backwards as the male dancer stays basically in one spot on the stage. A few couples doing this and modifications of this center stage, with the rest of the group doing the calisthenics, will make for an active verse.

And if you don't know what to do on the refrain, you haven't been to a baseball stadium in a while. (Hint: SPELL IT! with your body)

80s Footloose

Dance in the '80s turned up the heat a bit with songs like "Footloose." Its incredible energy and athleticism challenged Disco to take on break dancing acrobatics and cut a new kind of rug. Therefore, when staging this number, I always like to find out if there are any real acrobats in the group that we can utilize to add the kind of explosive theatrics the song calls for.

Working into the Floor: One of the most important concepts to grasp in this style of dance is the difference between working into the floor as opposed to on top of it. Have your group try running across the stage on top of the floor and then run across the stage 'into' the floor. Hopefully, they will understand that to run 'into' the floor involves staying close to it with bent knees and a sense of the energy going down as opposed to up.

U-Step: (Definition #444) Keeping your body square to the audience, perform a step touch pattern (step together). As you step, bend your knees and as you bring your feet together, straighten your legs so that the body has made a 'U' in the air. Remember to work 'into' the floor to make the move powerful. This simple step will be a good one for much of the verse in "Footloose."

Break Dance: Break Dancing covers a wide array of stunts from hip hop to popping, to rolling around on the floor like a top. For the most part it is very individualized and relies heavily on each dancer trying to 'out do' the next. What an easy way to stage a number! Let your dancers do their best to 'out do' each other on the dance floor while the rest of the group dances 'into' the floor around and behind them.

Conclusion

Hopefully some of these tips will help you in your staging of **Dance Hits Through the Decades.** In the Twenty-First Century we are lucky to have many visual resources, (i.e. movies, MTV, DVD's and more) to study and borrow ideas from. I'm sure you will find plenty of ideas that will enhance each of these numbers and you will have a rewarding time putting them together into effective routines. Hopefully through it all we will enjoy revisiting the moves that reflect the mentality of the dancers of yesteryear.

1955 Fun Facts

50s

"ROCK AROUND THE CLOCK"

- Recorded by Bill Haley and His Comets
- #1 hit record in 1955
- 24 weeks on the chart
- Featured in the movie *The Blackboard Jungle*
- Grammy Hall of Fame winner in 1982

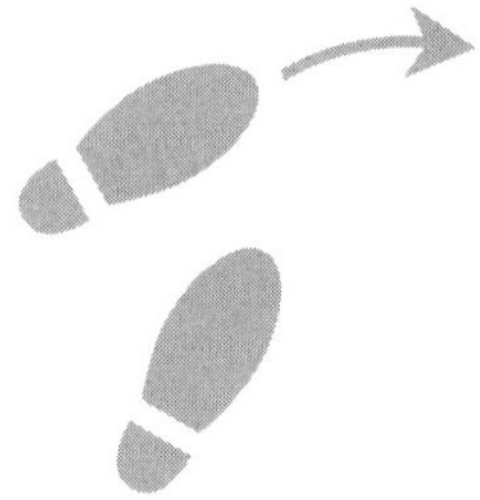

FILM AND TV IN 1955

- Adventures of Davy Crockett popular TV series and fashion showcase (for coonskin hats)
- Mary Martin appears as Peter Pan on TV
- Debuts on TV of Gunsmoke, Captain Kangaroo, The Mickey Mouse Club
- Movie *The Blackboard Jungle* first to use a new style of music: rock 'n' roll
- Musical *Oklahoma!* hits the big screen
- Best Picture Academy Award to *Marty*
- Actor James Dean dies in a highway crash

More About . . . "ROCK AROUND THE CLOCK"

Bill Haley (1925 - 1981) was born William John Clifton Haley, Jr. in Highland Park, Michigan. He led country and western groups in the 1940s and early 1950s with names like the Down Homers, the Four Aces of Western Swing, and the Saddlemen. He renamed his group the Comets in 1952 and recorded their first song called "Rock the Joint." The influence of country and western was present even in "Rock Around the Clock" with the use of a steel guitar on the record.

Bill Haley and His Comets were the #1 artists of the year in 1955. Rock and roll was just beginning its reign of popularity. The Comets were followed by some performers who were definitely not "rock and rollers" like Tennessee Ernie Ford, Mitch Miller, Roger Williams, Frank Sinatra, and Nat "King" Cole.

In 1955, it was estimated that the Comets would earn more than $500,000 for just their performances. They were the first American rock group to tour the United Kingdom. Bill Haley was inducted into the Rock and Roll Hall of Fame in 1987.

What Happened in 1955?

50s

THE WORLD

- Polio vaccine given to millions of youngsters
- Winston Churchill resigns as Prime Minister of Britain
- Disneyland opens in Anaheim, CA
- Volkswagen sells over a million Beetles which they had been making since 1936
- Colonel Sanders begins Kentucky Fried Chicken restaurant chain
- Albert Einstein dies at the age of 76

SPORTS

- Willie Mays hits 51 homers
- Brooklyn Dodgers win their first World Series
- Sugar Ray Robinson wins middleweight boxing crown

MUSIC

- 45s replaces 78s as preferred type of record
- Jukebox costs increase from a nickel to a dime per play
- Latin American dance craze, the Mambo, becomes popular
- "Cherry Pink and Apple Blossom White," a Latin-style song by Perez Prado, is the #1 song of the year
- Pat Boone has his Top 20 debut with "Ain't That a Shame" which is a cover version of a song recorded by Fats Domino
- The first national exposure for R&B (Rhythm and Blues) is on the Ed Sullivan Show

50s

Rock Around the Clock

Arranged by
ROGER EMERSON

Words and Music by MAX C. FREEDMAN
and JIMMY DeKNIGHT

*Harmony parts optional

join be - hind, _ we'll have some fun when the clock strikes one. We're gon - na
13
B♭9
F6
rock a - round the clock to - night, we're gon - na rock, rock, rock, 'til the
C9
B♭9
broad day - light. Gon - na rock, gon - na rock a - round _ the clock _ to - night! _
F6
21
When the clock strikes two, three and four _ if the
When it's eight, nine, ten, 'lev - en, too, _ I'll be

B♭9
band slows down we'll yell for more. We're gon - na rock a - round the
go - in' strong and so will you.
F6
clock to - night, we're gon - na rock, rock, rock, 'til the broad day - light. Gon - na
C9
B♭9
F6
rock, gon - na rock a - round the clock to - night!
33
"Dance Break"

B♭9
F6
37
C9
(2nd time)
To Coda
F6
When the
41
45
D.S. al Coda
chimes ring five, six and sev - en, we'll be right in sev-enth hea - ven. Gon-na
45
CODA
F6
ff
51
When the clock strikes twelve we'll
ff
49

pool our friends, start a rock - in' round the clock a - gain. We're gon - na
52
B♭9
55
F6
rock a - round the clock to - night! We're gon - na rock, rock, rock, 'til the
55
C9
B♭9
F6
N.C.
broad day - light. Gon - na rock, gon - na rock a - round _ the clock __ to - night! _
58
F13
opt. div.
opt. shake
Yeah! __
On cue 8va
62

Rock Around the Clock

LESSON PLAN AND ACTIVITIES

One of the most recognizable elements in "Rock Around the Clock" is the **rhythm** (a pattern of sound and silence with a beat) at the beginning. Ask students to clap the **accented** (stressed) notes as the introduction is played.

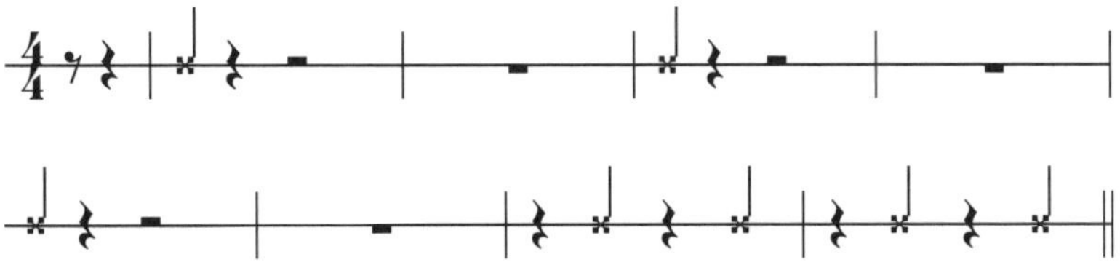

There are three **pitches** (the highness or lowness of musical sounds) in the introduction's **melody** (the "tune" of a song). Have students sing them or play them on a piano or guitar.

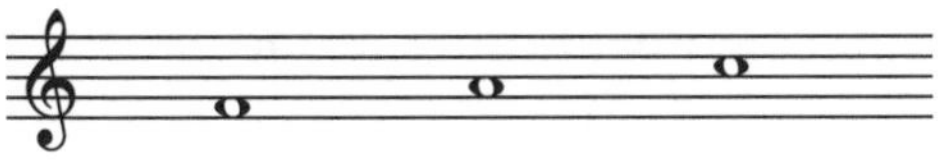

They can be identified by their letter names (F, A, and C) or by their place in the **scale** (a set of pitches in a specific order) which is do, mi, and sol or 1, 3, and 5.

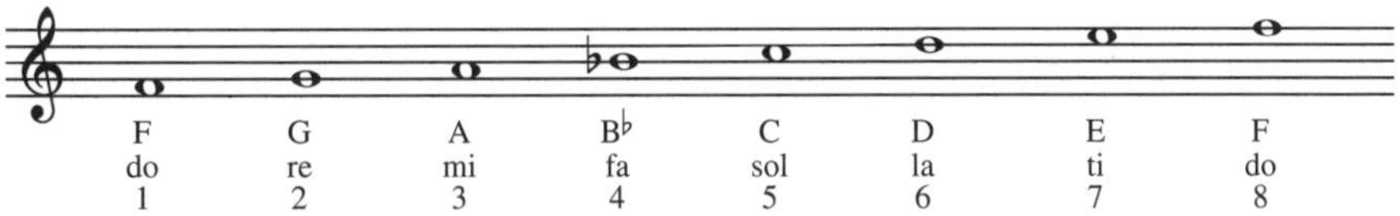

Have students find these three pitches in the introduction and sing them with letter names, syllables, or numbers. In what order do they first appear in the melody of "Rock Around the Clock"? *(F, A, C)*

Three or more pitches sung or played at the same time is called a **chord.** When the pitches from the introduction of "Rock Around the Clock" are put together, they look like this:

Have students play these chords on a piano, guitar or classroom instrument.

Now have students sing the chord. Divide into three groups. One group sings the lowest pitch (F), the 2nd group sings the middle pitch (A), and the 3rd group sings the highest pitch (C).

A chord gets its name from the **root,** or lowest pitch, which in this case is F Major.

There are three chords in the **accompaniment** (the supporting music in the background) of "Rock Around the Clock." They are the first (I), fourth (IV), and fifth (V) chords in the **key** (the tonal center of a song) of F major.

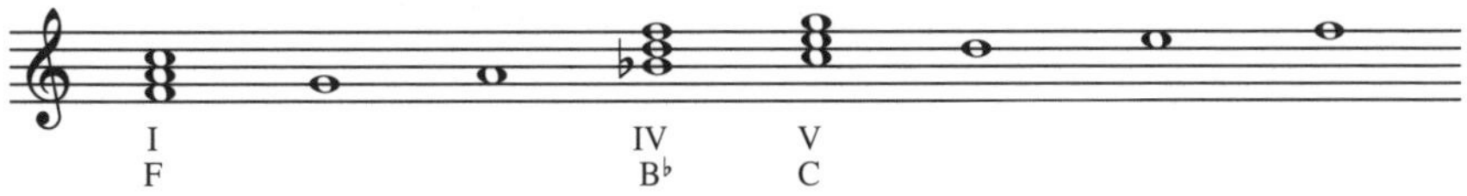

Have students practice playing these chords on piano, guitar, or classroom instruments in this order:

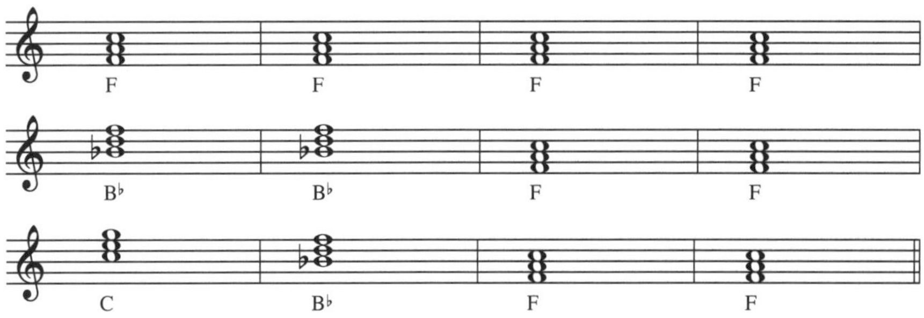

Tell students they are playing the **chord progression** (a sequence of one chord after another) to "Rock Around the Clock." Have them play this chord progression beginning at measure 9 to accompany the rest of the song.

Another way to play a chord progression is one pitch at a time. Play these pitches in the lower section of the piano or guitar. Do students recognize them? *(They are the pitches of the I, IV and V chords.)* This is an example of a bass part for the accompaniment.

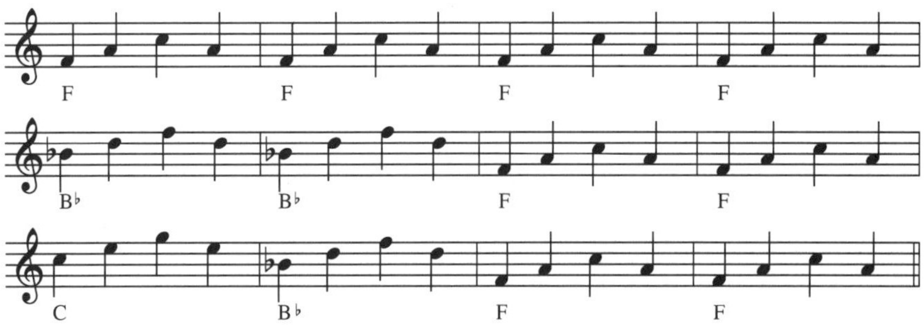

Have the students accompany "Rock Around the Clock" by playing the chords on guitars, the piano or other barred classroom instruments and the bass part in the lower portion of the instruments.

✶ Can students follow the **road map** to this arrangement? The arranger, Roger Emerson, decided to use *a dal segno al coda* (D.S. al Coda) which is an Italian term for repeating a section of the song before singing the ending section (Coda).

Here is the order of the song:
- sing up to the D.S. al Coda (measure 48);
- go back to the D.S. (𝄋) at measure 13 and repeat through measure 42 (using the lower set of lyrics at measure 20);
- at the (2nd time) To Coda 𝄌 (measure 42), skip to the Coda (measure 49) and sing to the end.

Have students follow the 'roadmap' before singing the song. Have someone play, or use the recording and stop somewhere in the middle. Have students point to the place in the music where it stopped. Sing through the song when students can follow its overall **form.**

1962 Fun Facts

60s

"THE LOCO-MOTION"

- Recorded by Little Eva in 1962
- Debut on the charts June 30
- Peaked at #1
- 16 weeks on the charts
- #1 hit for Grand Funk Railroad in 1974

FILM AND TV IN 1962

- Walter Cronkite begins as anchorman of the CBS Evening News
- Popular TV shows include The Beverly Hillbillies, Candid Camera, and Bonanza
- Johnny Carson starts to host The Tonight Show
- *How the West Was Won, The Longest Yard,* and *The Music Man* are popular movies
- Gregory Peck wins an Oscar as best actor in *To Kill a Mockingbird*
- Actress Marilyn Monroe dies

More About . . . "THE LOCO-MOTION"

Little Eva (Eva Narcissus Boyd) was babysitting for songwriters Carole King and Gerry Goffin in their New Jersey home. She began to do a dance in an up-and-down motion as the two were working on a song called "The Loco-motion." This was the beginning of not only a dance craze, but also combined the song with its first recording artist.

The Locomotion joined dances like the Twist, Pony, Mashed Potato and Watusi that were popular in 1962. Many of these dances were featured on an afternoon TV dance show called American Bandstand. It was hosted by Dick Clark who would go on to host many other television shows and New Year's Eve festivities.

"The Loco-motion" was nominated for a Grammy Award as Best R & B recording. R & B was a term first used in 1949 by Billboard magazine to categorize the style of music, Rhythm and Blues. The 1974 version of "The Loco-motion" by Grand Funk Railroad stayed on the charts for 20 weeks, even longer than Little Eva's 16 weeks.

What Happened in 1962?

60s

THE WORLD

- John F. Kennedy is elected president
- John Glenn orbits the earth
- The World's Fair is in Seattle, WA with its "space" theme
- A blockade of Cuba is in place because of Soviet ballistic missiles
- Algeria becomes an independent country after more than 100 years of French rule
- Andy Warhol exhibits his pop art in New York City

SPORTS

- Philadelphia's Wilt Chamberlain scores 100 points in one basketball game and averages 50 points per game for the season
- Sonny Liston is the world heavyweight boxing champion
- The Green Bay Packers wins the NFL title (no Super Bowl yet!)
- Brazil wins the World Cup
- Arnold Palmer has his finest year as a golfer

MUSIC

- The Twist becomes a dance popularized by Chubby Checker who appears in the movie, *Twist Around the Clock*
- The Beatles sing before a record-size crowd of 900 at the Cavern Club
- Ringo Starr replaces drummer Pete Best in The Beatles
- Elvis Presley's movie, *Blue Hawaii,* is No. 1 for 20 weeks
- Record singles sell for $.98 while albums are $3.98 (mono) and $4.98 (stereo)
- Original rock and roll disc jockey Alan Freed is fined $300 for payola
- The #1 record of the year is "I Can't Stop Loving You" by Ray Charles
- Herb Albert records "The Lonely Bull" for $65 in his garage

The Loco-Motion

Arranged by
MARK A. BRYMER

Words and Music by
GERRY GOFFIN and CAROLE KING

*Harmony parts optional

E♭
Cm
13
A♭
Come on baby do the lo-co-mo-tion.
My lit-tle ba-by sis-ter can
There's nev-er been a dance that's so
Fm
A♭
F7
f
do it with ease. It's eas-i-er than learn-in' your A. B. C.'s
eas-y to do. It ev-en makes you hap-py when you're feel-in' blue,
So
E♭
B♭
To Coda
E♭
mf
come on, come on, do the lo-co-mo-tion with me! You got-ta
f
mf
20
A♭
E♭
swing your hips now. Come on ba-by, jump up, jump back.

B♭7
27
N.C.
Clap
Oh well, I think you got the knack. Oh ba-by won't you do the lo-co-mo-tion,
D.S. al Coda
do the lo - co-mo-tion. Do the lo-co-mo-tion, do the lo - co-mo-tion.
CODA
E♭
C
3 fr
32
F
N.C.
Clap
Group 2
mf
me! Do the lo-co-mo-tion, do the lo - co-mo-tion. Do the lo-co-mo-tion,
Group 1
F
Dm
Move a-round the floor in a lo-co-mo-tion. Come on ba-by do
Group 2
do the lo - co-mo-tion. Do the lo - co-mo-tion, do the lo - co-mo-tion. Come on ba-by do

F
Dm
the lo - co - mo - tion. Do it hold - in' hands if you get the no - tion.
the lo - co - mo - tion. Do the lo - co - mo - tion, do the lo - co - mo - tion.
39
F
Dm
B♭
Group 1
Group 2
44
Come on ba - by do the lo - co - mo - tion. Do it nice and eas - y now,
cresc.
42
Gm
3fr
B♭
G7
f
don't lose com - trol. A lit - tle bit of rhy - thm and a lot of soul. So
f
45
F
C
F
50
Clap
me!
come on come on do the lo - co - mo - tion with Do the lo - co - mo - tion,
48

Dm F Dm
do the lo - co-mo-tion. Come on ba-by do the lo-co-mo-tion.
51
F Dm F Dm
Clap
Do the lo-co-mo-tion, do the lo - co-mo-tion. Come on ba-by do
54
58
F Dm
the lo-co-mo-tion. Come on ba-by do the lo-co-mo-tion.
57
B♭ F/C C F/C B♭/C N.C. F
Come on ba-by do the lo-co-mo-tion. Lo-co-mo - tion!
60

The Loco-Motion

LESSON PLAN AND ACTIVITIES

Rhythm plays an important role in the song, "The Loco-motion," (as it does with most rock music). Have students locate the following 'clapping' rhythm in the music:

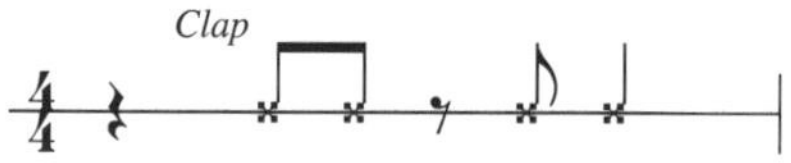

One way to learn a rhythm is to think of words that fit the notes. Here is one possibility:

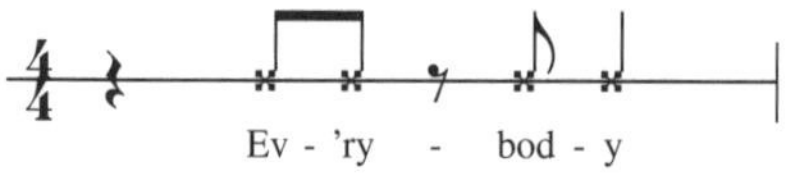

Or think of someone's name that has the correct number of syllables. For example:

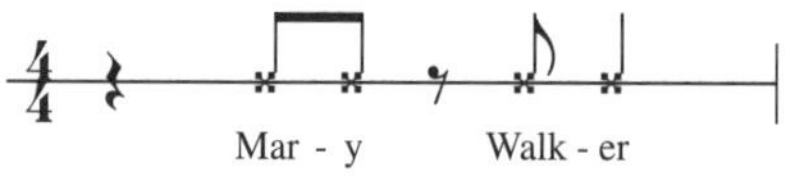

or

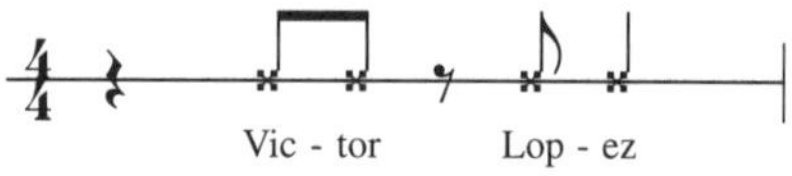

Is there anyone in the class with a four-syllable name? Have students say his or her name as they clap the rhythm. Then just clap the rhythm and 'think' the names. Finally, see if the class can clap the rhythm by looking at the music.

Point out the **repeat signs** in measure 1 and 4.

They tell the singer to perform the material in between the signs twice. The instruction '2nd time only' is written above the singing part, which tells the singer to begin singing when those measures repeat the 'second time'.

The **melody** of "The Loco-motion" starts with pitches that move up and down by **step.** Have students sing the following pitches or play them on a piano or classroom intrument.

Ask students to find these pitches in the music. *(measures 5 & 9)*

A **sequence** of these pitches occurs at measure 13. This is where the same pattern is played or sung at a different pitch level. Have students sing or play these pitches after they have located them in measure 13.

Do they see how the pattern is the same but the pitches are different from the first example?

✶ The opposite of steps are **leaps** where the **interval** (or distance between pitches) is greater than a step. The example below shows a 'leap' from one pitch to another. Have students find these two notes in the melody. *(last pitch in measure 16 and first pitch in measure 17)*

Ask students to find more examples of leaps in the melody of "The Loco-motion."

Have the class find this example of steps and leaps in "The Loco-motion" *(measures 16 & 17)* and identify the steps and leaps. *(leap, step, leap, leap, step)*

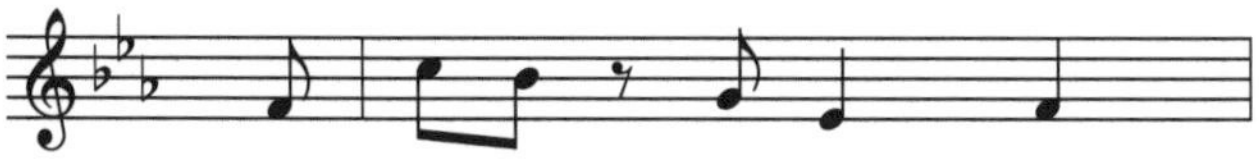

✶ The **form** of this arrangement is similar to "Rock Around the Clock." Point out the dal segno al coda signs. See if students can follow its form by asking them to fill in the blanks below with the correct answers.

1. Repeat measures *(1)* through *(4)* at the beginning.
2. Sing up to the D.S. al Coda at the end of measure *(30)*.
3. Go back to the D.S. sign (𝄋) at measure *(5)*.
4. Sing measures *(5)* through *(18)* (using the lower set of lyrics) until you see To Coda 𝄌 at measure *(18)*.
5. Skip to the Coda which is measure *(31)* to the end.

Have students locate all of the places where they are to clap. Combine the singing with the handclapping as you do "The Loco-motion."

1979 Fun Facts

70s

"Y.M.C.A."

- First released in October of 1978, but also popular in 1979
- Recorded by The Village People
- Peaked at #2 which was the highest ranking for any Village People record
- On the charts for 26 weeks and sold over a million copies

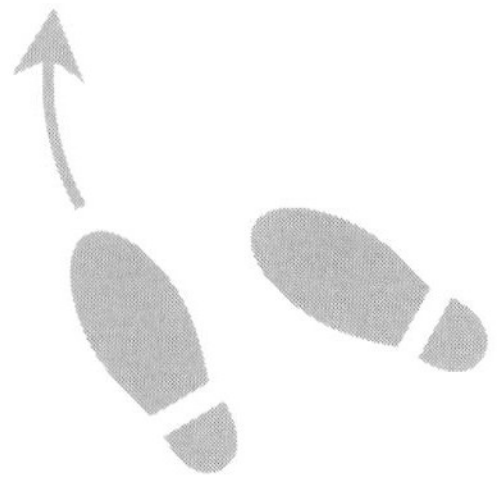

FILM AND TV IN 1979

- Popular TV shows include 60 Minutes, Three's Company, and M*A*S*H
- Videotapes are used to sell rock music like Queen's "Bohemian Rhapsody"
- *Kramer vs. Kramer* wins Academy Awards as Best Picture and Dustin Hoffman wins as Best Actor
- Some controversial movies are *Apocalypse Now* and *The China Syndrome*

More About . . . "Y.M.C.A."

The Village People were formed by French producer Jacques Morali in 1977. There were six members of the group who dressed in costumes to represent different types of people: a policeman, cowboy, construction worker, Indian chief, biker, and G.I. (enlisted person in the U.S. Army). The group was based in New York City but performed all over the world.

Other hits by The Village People include "Macho Man" and "In the Navy." They appeared in the 1980 movie, *Can't Stop the Music* and were ranked as the #4 recording artists in 1979.

Probably the most memorable element of "Y. M. C. A." is the motions that acompany the song title when it is sung in the chorus (the repeated section of the song). Each letter (y, m, c, a) is imitated with the placement of arms and bodies so that it looks like the letter as it is sung in the song.

What Happened in 1979?

70s

THE WORLD

- Mother Teresa wins the Nobel Peace Prize
- The U.S. Surgeon General warns that cigarette smoking causes cancer
- President Carter flies to the Middle East to finalize terms of the peace treaty between Israel and Egypt
- Gas rationing begins when oil prices are ten times higher than in 1973
- Margaret Thatcher is elected as the first woman Prime Minister in Britain
- The U.S. Congress loans money to the struggling Chrysler Corporation
- Pioneer II gets close enough to Saturn to take photographs

SPORTS

- Pittsburgh Steelers win the Super Bowl in a close game over Dallas
- Michigan State's basketball team with Magic Johnson wins the NCAA championship over Larry Bird's Indiana State
- Bjorn Borg wins his fourth Wimbledon tennis title
- Seattle Supersonics win the NBA championship

MUSIC

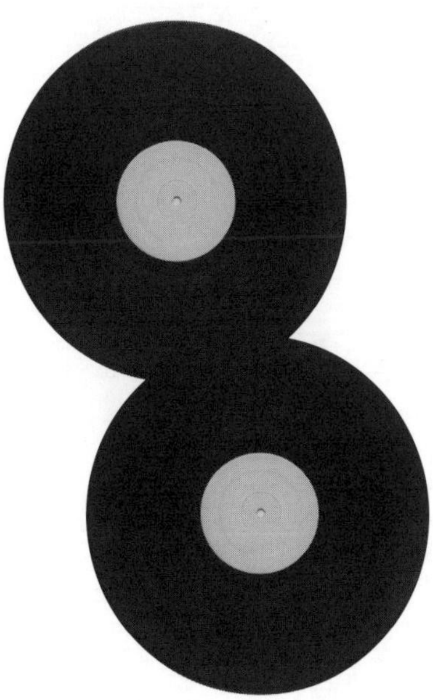

- The #1 record of the year is "My Sharona" by The Knack
- Rap music, sometimes called "hiphop," is introduced to the world with "Rapper's Delight" by The Sugarhill Gang
- It now takes $350,00 to $500,000 to produce and promote a record album
- Digital recording begins when used by Stephen Stills
- Paul McCartney signs a $20 million deal with Columbia Records
- 50% of the highest rated radio stations are broadcasting in FM

70s

Y.M.C.A.

Arranged by
ROGER EMERSON

Words and Music by JACQUES MORALI,
HENRI BELOLO and VICTOR WILLIS

*Harmony parts optional

A♭ Gm Fm E♭
15
un - hap - py. Young man, there's a place you can go. ___ I said,
this one thing: No man does it all by him - self. ___ I said,
was so jive. That's when some-one came up to me ___ and said,
14
Cm A♭
young man, when you're short on your dough, _ you can stay there and I'm
young man, put your pride on the shelf ___ and just go there to the
young man, take a walk up the street, _ it's a place there called the
17
B♭/D A♭/C B♭ A♭ Gm Fm A♭(add9)/B♭
sure you will find _ man - y ways to ___ have a good time.
Y. M. C. A. ___ I'm sure they can ___ help you to - day.
Y. M. C. A. ___ they can start you ___ back on your way.
20
f
E♭ Cm
f
25
It's fun to stay at the Y. M. C. A! It's fun to stay at the Y. M. C. A!
24

Fm
Fm(maj7)
Fm7
They have ev - er - y - thing for young men to en - joy, you can
28
Ab/Bb
Eb
33
hang-out with all the boys. It's fun to stay at the Y. M. C. A! It's fun to stay at the
31
Cm
Fm
Fm(maj7)
Fm7
Y. M. C. A! You can get your-self clean, you can have a good meal, you can
35
Ab/Bb
1,2
3
do what-ev - er you feel. It's fun to stay at the
39

E♭
Cm
Y. M. C. A! It's fun to stay at the Y. M. C. A! They have
Fm
Fm(maj7)
Fm7
A♭/B♭
ev - er - y - thing for young men to en - joy, you can hang-out with all the boys!
A♭maj7/B♭
It's fun to stay at the...
A♭/B♭
E♭6
E♭
E♭6/B♭
E♭
ff
Y. M. C. A!

Y.M.C.A.

LESSON PLAN AND ACTIVITIES

The form of "Y.M.C.A." is organized into **verses** and a **refrain.** A verse is the "story" part of a song where the pitches stay the same but the **lyrics** *(words)* are different. There are three verses in "Y.M.C.A." Have students locate them. What are the first words of each verse? *(Young man)*

The refrain (sometimes called the **chorus**) is repeated several times. It has the same lyrics and pitches and usually includes the title of the song. Ask the class to find the refrain of "Y.M.C.A."

This arrangement also uses **repeat signs.** Have the class find them. *(The first repeat sign appears at measure 7 and the second at the end of measure 40.)* You are to repeat the material inbetween these signs.

This arrangement uses **first, second,** and **third endings.**

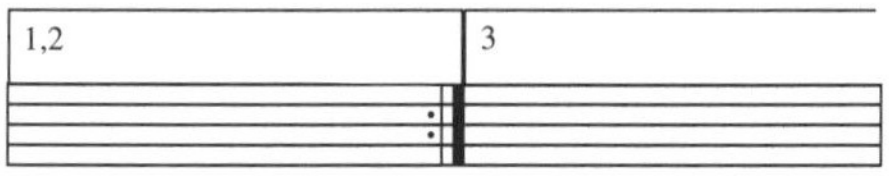

Ask students if they can explain how to use these endings. *(Sing the notes in the 1,2 ending the first time; then repeat back to measure 7 and sing the second verse. When you come to this ending the second time, sing it again, and once again repeat back to measure 7 and sing the third verse. When you get to the 1,2 ending the third time, skip this ending and sing the 3rd ending. Go on to sing the rest of the song.)*

Here is one of the most recognizable rhythms in "Y.M.C.A.":

Ask the class to find this rhythm in the song. How many times does this rhythm appear? *(7 without repeats)*

Does the melody of "Y.M.C.A." begin with a step or a leap? *(leap)*

There is sequence in the melody, with leaps at different pitch levels.

Have the class sing the pitches, then play them on classroom instruments.

Ask students to locate these leaps in the melody *(at the beginning of measures 7, 9, 11, 15, 17, 19)* and tell the class to watch for them as they sing the melody of "Y.M.C.A."

1984 Fun Facts

80s

"FOOTLOOSE"

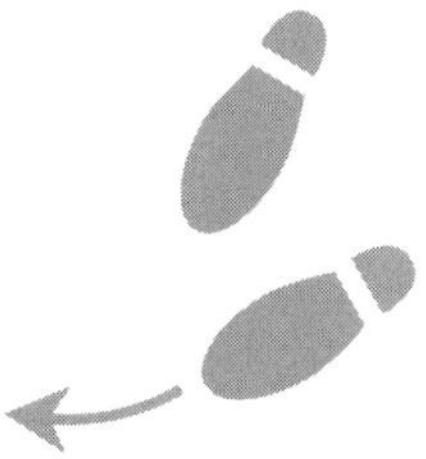

- Featured on the soundtrack for the film with the same name
- Recorded by Kenny Loggins
- Debut on the charts in January
- Peaked at #1
- All song lyrics for the movie were written by the movie's screenwriter, Dean Pitchford
- #4 song of the year

FILM AND TV IN 1984

- Popular TV shows are Dynasty, Dallas, The Cosby Show, and Family Ties
- Soundtrack for *Purple Rain* by Prince sells a million copies in the first week
- Popular movies are *Ghostbusters, Indiana Jones and the Temple of Doom, Gremlins*, and *The Karate Kid*
- *Amadeus* wins an Academy Award for Best Picture

More About . . . "FOOTLOOSE"

Music in the movies became popular once again in the mid 80s with hits like "Footloose" and "Flashdance." The soundtracks helped to promote the films and vice versa. Kenny Loggins sang the title song to *Footloose* which was released in February of 1984. It would rank as the fourth most popular musical rented in the 1980s. *Footloose* was later produced as a Broadway musical which ran from 1998 to 2000. Based on the screenplay, it follows the character Ren McCormack who moves to a small town where dancing is not allowed. Of course, Ren would change that.

Loggins was born in 1947 in Everett, WA, and has been successful as a recording artist as well as a song writer. He wrote "House at Pooh Corner" which was recorded by the Nitty Gritty Dirt Band. Signing as a solo artist in 1971, Loggins went on to form the group Loggins and Messina with Jim Messina. Their biggest hit was "Your Mama Don't Dance" (they also didn't think your daddy would rock and roll). Other hits by Kenny Loggins include "Danger Zone" and "I'm Alright." It is his infectious song about the need to dance that has been most popular.

What Happened in 1984?

80s

THE WORLD

- Global warming is cited because of the "greenhouse" effect caused by gasses such as carbon dioxide
- The phrase "yuppies" is used to describe young upwardly-mobile professionals
- Ronald Reagan wins re-election as President
- Bell Telephone is broken up by a court order
- Break Dancing becomes a national fad
- Geraldine Ferraro is selected as the first woman vice presidential nominee of a major party
- 15 million Americans own videocassette recorders
- U.S. Marines are pulled out of Lebanon

SPORTS

- The Olympics are held in Los Angeles with sprinter Carl Lewis, hurdler Edwin Moses, and gymnast Mary Lou Retton
- The Los Angeles Raiders with the Super Bowl
- John McEnroe and Martina Navratilova win Wimbledon and the U.S. Open tennis titles
- The University of Miami are national football champions

MUSIC

- Bruce Springsteen's *Born in the U.S.A.* is a best-selling album in Britain and the U.S.
- Lionel Richie sings "All Night Long" to 2.6 billion TV viewers for the opening ceremonies of the Olympic Games
- The Jackson's Victory tour is the top grossing tour of the year, earning $4.5 million in 3 days at Giant's Stadium
- Michael Jackson's *Thriller* sells 30 million copies world wide, becoming the biggest selling record ever
- CD sales reach $4.2 million

80s

Footloose

Arranged by
KIRBY SHAW

Words by DEAN PITCHFORD
and KENNY LOGGINS
Music by KENNY LOGGINS

* *ascending smear — slide into note from one-half step below.*
** *fall-off — descending vocal slide.*

* Harmony parts optional

F Bb Gm/Gb F F Gm/E
41
ise, pull me off of my knees. Jack, get
rie, shake it, shake it for me. Whoa, Mi-
38
F Bb Gm/Gb F Gm/E
back, come on be-fore we crack.
lo, come on, come on, let's go.
Lose your
42
F
To Coda
1
Eb Bb F7 Cm/F
All clap
blues, ev-'ry bod-y cut foot-loose.
46
Bb/F F7 Fm7 Gm/F F Bb/C
2
Eb Bb
ev-'ry-bod-y cut foot-
49

F
F13
All clap
53
2nd time only
cut foot - loose, Woh,
cut foot - loose, woh.
1st time only
loose.
Woh,
woh.
53
N.C.
57
Claps cont. to m. 70
Group I Group II
First, you've got to turn me a - round.
(I) (II)
Sec - ond, and put your feet
57
8vb to end
(All)
on the ground.
Third, now take a hold of your soul.
60
C
C7
Ah.
63

C
C7
C
C7
End claps
mf
cresc.
f
D.S. al Coda
Oh, I'm turn-in' it
67
CODA
All clap
Eb
Bb/D
ev - 'ry bod - y cut, ev - 'ry bod - y cut, ev - 'ry bod - y cut, ev - 'ry -
71
Eb
Bb/D
Bb
Shout
mf
f
bod - y cut, ev - 'ry - bod - y cut, ev - 'ry - bod - y cut, ev - 'ry - bod - y
74
Eb
Bb
F7
Cm/F
Bb/F
F7
F
Shout
ev - 'ry - bod - y cut foot loose.
ff
77

Footloose

LESSON PLAN AND ACTIVITIES

At the beginning of this arrangement of "Footloose," singers are to clap one of the most widely-used rhythms in rock music ... the **off beat.** This is an example of **syncopation** where a rhythmic **accent** (emphasized or louder) is placed on a 'weak' beat or part of a beat. (Beats one and three are considered the 'strong' beats; beats two and four are the 'weak' beats.) Have students clap this rhythm, then transfer to non-pitched instruments (for example, tambourine or claves).

Here is another syncopated rhythm that was clapped in one of the other arrangements. What song included this rhythm? *(The Loco-motion)*

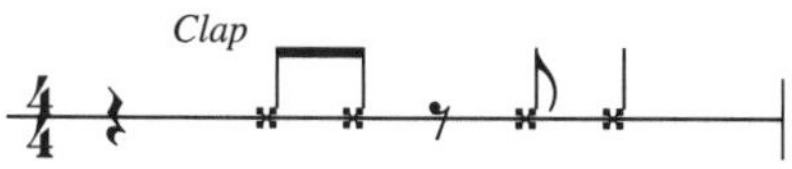

Have students clap this rhythm, then transfer to non-pitched instruments.

Now combine these two syncopated rhythms. Have the class clap them, play them on instruments, or clap one rhythm and play the other on instruments. Repeat the combined rhythms several times.

Another example of a syncopated rhythm begins in the melody at measure 57 of "Footloose." Have students tap their foot to the beat as they clap the rhythm example below. The arrows above the music represent the placement of your foot ("down" or "up") as each note is clapped. Tell the students that **upbeats** (or the weak part of the beat) occur when your foot is "up" while tapping the beat. How many times does this rhythm land on an upbeat? *(5)*

Have the class sing measures 57 and 58 once they have clapped the rhythm. When that rhythm is secure, have them clap the rhythm of the melody in measures 59 and 60 and then in measures 61 and 62. Sing those measures once students can clap the rhythm. Reading rhythms is an essential step in reading music.

The **form** (or 'road map') to this arrangement of "Footloose" is rather involved. The song uses **repeat signs** (with **first and second endings**) and **dal segno (D.S.) al coda.**

Have students look at the overall form of "Footloose" and fill in the blanks below with the correct answers.

1. Start at the beginning clapping hands through measure *(8)*.
2. Begin singing at measure *(9)* and continue up through the first ending to the repeat sign at measure *(51)*.
3. Repeat back to measure *(9)* (singing the lower set of lyrics) and continue up through measure *(46)* .
4. Skip the first ending and sing the second ending beginning at measure *(52)*.
5. Repeat measures *(53)* through *(56)* ; add the clapping rhythm both times; add the top vocal line the *(2nd)* time through.
6. Sing measures *(57)* through *(70)* , along with the clapping rhythm until you see D.S. al Coda at measure *(70)*.
7. Jump back to the D.S. sign (𝄋) at measure *(33)*.
8. Sing measures *(33)* through *(46)* (using the upper set of lyrics) until you see To Coda 𝄌 at measure *(46)*.
9. Jump to the Coda at measure *(71)* and sing to the end.

Point out that if a notehead has an "x," the word is spoken instead of sung. Have students find the spoken rhythms. *(measures 57, 59, 61, 75, 76, 77, 78)*

Have the class find another 'clapping' rhythm in the Coda. *(measures 72 and 74)* On which beats do the students clap? *(3 and 4)*

Now combine all of these elements and sing "Footloose."